Advance Praise for *Poem*

"Beautiful, heart-felt poems for connecting with the Earth."

—Joseph Bharat Cornell, author of *Sharing Nature* and *Deep Nature Play: A Guide to Wholeness, Aliveness, Creativity, and Inspired Learning.*

"Brimming with insight and imagination, Kai Siedenburg's debut collection of poems explores our relationship to nature in provocative ways. The Earth runs a personal ad, we envision our own inner light as seen by someone on a distant planet, we feel what it is to make love to the Earth. To spend time with this collection is like sitting by a pure mountain stream; we are filled with peace, wonder, and delight. These inspiring poems and simple practices will help you deepen your connection with nature wherever you are."

—Mary Reynolds Thompson, author of *Embrace Your Inner Wild: 52 Reflections for an Eco-Centric World* and *Reclaiming the Wild Soul: How Earth's Landscapes Restore Us to Wholeness.*

"I've been sharing Kai's poems with my students and workshop participants for years. I love how they help people to see the natural world more clearly and appreciate it more profoundly. From the simple, sensual invitation of 'bare feet on the Earth,' to the passionate 'they can't keep us apart,' her poems invite us into a more intimate relationship with all of life."

—Ariana Candell, LMFT, R-DMT, Ecotherapist and Founder of The Earthbody Institute

"Kai Siedenburg asks something that would have never occurred to me, but will from now on: 'What do trees think about in the morning?' She believes in the wisdom of the wild within each of us, celebrates our inability 'to hold our tongues,' expressing faith in our human nature to speak out in honor of the earth… What I want from poetry is what Kai gives me, to see anew and to feel deeply, to be reminded of who I am. As she sees the earth do, she gives her poems everything she's got. Brava, Kai Siedenburg, Brava!"

—Patrice Vecchione, author of *Step into Nature: Nurturing Imagination & Spirit in Everyday Life*

Poems of Earth and Spirit:

70 Poems and 40 Practices
to Deepen Your Connection with Nature

by Kai Siedenburg

illustrated by Christi Voenell

 Our Nature Connection

OurNatureConnection.com

PoemsofEarthandSpirit.com

for all my relations,
and for the benefit of all beings

The trees,
the stones,
the water,
the birds...

Everything
speaks
to me.

And
I listen.

CONTENTS

INTRODUCTION

Poetry and Me:
an Unexpected Love Story

Poems are
wild creatures,

with minds and timing
all their own.

Sometimes,
when I am
quiet and still,

they come to me
like wild birds,

thrilling me
with their
unexpected grace,

colorful wings,
and mysterious songs.

    The first poems I wrote appeared quite suddenly, like buds opening in the spring. They arrived spontaneously and effortlessly, as though they had been eagerly waiting for someone to give them form. Some people would say I wrote them, but truthfully the poems were writing themselves through me.

    I was honored yet surprised that they had chosen me. While I loved reading poetry, I hadn't written it as an adult, nor aspired to. With no formal instruction beyond a few hours in high school, I didn't exactly appear qualified, by conventional standards, to write poetry. Fortunately for me, poems are not overly concerned with protocol. Apparently they saw some raw potential that they could work with.

I believe the poems came to me because I had immersed myself in listening deeply to nature. Without realizing it, I had rolled out a giant red carpet that announced, "welcome, poems!"—and a large contingent of them appeared at my doorstep.

They arrived during a time of great transition in my life. For 25 years I had worked with remarkable people and organizations on causes I believed in, primarily promoting sustainable and socially just food systems. It was a meaningful and rewarding vocation, but in 2010 it became clear that it was time to serve in a different way.

I knew this was not merely a career change, but a call to discover my true purpose and share my deepest gifts. I needed to take a big step back from what I had been doing, learn to listen in new ways, and connect with a greater wisdom to find my next path. And to do that, I knew exactly where to go.

For as long as I can remember, I have loved being in nature. As a little girl, I enjoyed hiking, camping, and trips to the beach with my family. As an adult, I continued regular forays into the wild and discovered backpacking, cross-country skiing, kayaking, and more. Now, facing a life-changing transition, I felt called to relate to the natural world in different ways.

Instead of going out with friends and hiking at a steady clip, I was drawn to go solo, to hold still or move slowly, to be quiet and receptive. I still loved hiking, but now I also loved to settle into one place and listen. I would sit by a creek and watch the water flow, or lean into a tree and gaze up through the branches, falling under nature's spell and opening myself to whatever wanted to come.

I had a distinct sense that the natural world was speaking to me and inviting me to give voice to our deepening relationship. I could feel myself entering into a powerful and peaceful communion with something much greater than myself in a way that I had never experienced. I felt profoundly held and supported by the natural world, as if I was coming home to my true self and my larger family. I felt less alone and more connected than ever.

It was as though I had found a window to another world that had always been there, but that I hadn't seen. I knew that listening deeply to nature and sharing what I received was the essential foundation of my new path to service. It was not at all what I had anticipated, and yet it made perfect sense—it was what I had been preparing to do my entire life without realizing it.

I started guiding nature immersion programs in the redwood forests near my home in Santa Cruz, creating experiential journeys that invited people into deeper communion with the natural world. I was excited to witness and hear about the magic that these groups experienced: profound peace, creative inspiration, new insights, healing of old wounds. Even those who had spent a great deal of time in nature were experiencing it in new ways, finding their own windows to another world.

Listening to nature also transformed my approach to writing. I was well versed in writing with clear goals and deadlines—writing that got the job done. But the trees and birds taught me how to write in ways that completely re-wrote the job description. They taught me to write effortlessly, abundantly, and wildly, and it took me to surprising, delightful places.

The work flowed freely, as though it was coming directly from a limitless wellspring of creation. I spent many happy hours "alone" in nature, wandering or sitting quietly, listening for what wanted to come, and recording it in my trusty notebook. Over time, I received a vast and diverse body of work—poems, practices, classes, and more; mostly focused on inviting people into a deeper communion with the natural world.

Poetry and nature, I've discovered, have much in common. They are both patient and generous teachers who have taught me many things: to see the peace and beauty of the living world more clearly and feel it more deeply; to recognize trees, streams, and all beings as kind friends and wise elders; to listen and write in receptive, co-creative ways; and to trust myself and my voice.

My hope is that this book will help you find your own windows to a deep and nourishing connection with nature that will support and sustain you wherever you go.

A Few Words from the Poems

Welcome, dear reader!

It takes a special kind of person to find their way to a book like Poems of Earth and Spirit, and we are honored to meet you.

Now that you're here, we'd love to share a few things about ourselves…

We prefer to be savored, not gobbled. We are more delicious and nourishing when enjoyed one or a few at a time—like a box of gourmet chocolates or your favorite healthy treat.

We like to be read slowly or out loud, sometimes more than once to allow us to give our gifts more fully.

We appreciate quality one-on-one time with you and being shared with others.

We delight in going outside with you, especially into natural settings. We enjoy meadows, forests, streams, beaches, neighborhood parks—anywhere beautiful outdoors that you like to go. We love it when you take us on relaxing getaways and vacations.

We like going to bed with you. We like to lull you to sleep and nourish your dreams. We love to wake up next to you and see your beautiful, groggy face in the morning.

We cherish quiet moments with you. We appreciate having enough space to allow our ripples to spread into stillness. We are expansive spirits who don't like being rushed or compressed into cramped spaces.

Now that you know something about what we enjoy, we want to share why we're here...

We come in peace. We come in love. And we're on a mission. We are here:

> To bring more peace, joy, and healing into a troubled world.

> To help you rekindle your intrinsic bond with all life, and recognize all beings as potential friends and teachers.

> To inspire you to reclaim your innate connection with Earth and Spirit, and to deepen that connection for the benefit of all beings.

May these poems provide sustenance for your journey.

TREES

What Do Trees Think About in the Morning?

What do trees
think about
in the morning,

as the sun's golden light
touches each of their branches,
gently awakening them
to a new day?

Do they give thanks
just to be alive?

Do they lift their branches
in heartfelt gratitude
for the generous gifts
of this green earth,

for neighbors and friends
both near and far,
for the parents
who gave them life,
and the ancestors
who came before them?

Are they proud to be part
of a vast and ancient guild
of skilled artisans,

performing
the essential alchemy
of transmuting
sunlight, water, and air

into leaves and branches,
fruits and seeds,
and air for countless creatures
to breathe?

Is it thrilling
to work this everyday magic,
to create so much
from such simple materials?

How does it feel
to do this noble, essential work,
to give so much
to so many

and ask so little in return,
day after day,
year after year?

Do they ever
get tired of giving?

Do they ever
want to be
appreciated more?

What do trees think about
in the morning?

A Sweet Deal

Here's the deal,
says the tree
to the birds—

I'll give you
an abundant array
of perches,

breathtaking views
of the landscape,

a safe place
to raise
your babies,

and all the
fruit, seeds,
and bugs
you can eat.

All I ask
in return

is that
you sing
your song.

Among the Branches

Birds who
magically disappear
into the spaces
between the leaves

and, from the safety
of this leafy refuge,
send forth exultant songs
for all to hear;

Insects
going about
their daily labors,
small but essential players
in the great drama of life;

Spiders
weaving webs
that catch
sunlight and rainbows
as well as food;

Mosses
curled up
into themselves,
patiently awaiting
the next rainfall
to reveal
their lush green glory;

And a soft, sweet song
whenever the wind
comes to call.

Body of Work

A breath
of fresh air...

the respite
of cool shade
on a hot day...

gentle music
when the
wind stirs...

quiet beauty
that pleases the eye
and soothes
the spirit.

The surprising gift
of abundant blossoms
after an
apparently lifeless winter...

a bold display
of colors
in the fall...

All these
and much more
are part of

the vast
and beautiful
body of work
of trees—

the gathered acorns
and bushels
of apples
part of their
collected works;

the carved
and polished
tables and chairs
a retrospective—

one that usually endures
long beyond
the life of the
often anonymous
artists.

Becoming Tree

Sunlight

Entering leaves

Becoming tree

Becoming blossom

Becoming fruit

Becoming seed

Becoming tree

SEEING NATURE,
BEING NATURE

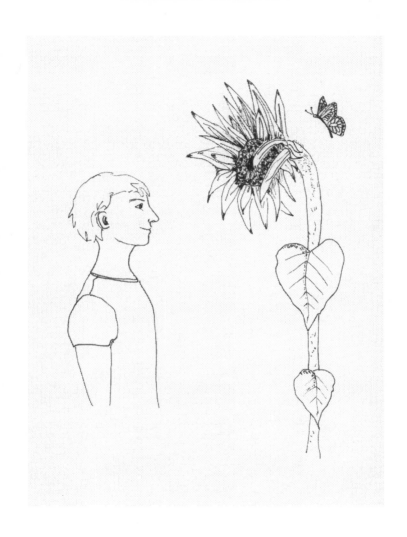

When I Was a Creek

When I was
a tree,

I sang and danced
with the wind
and offered
food and refuge
to all who came.

When I was
a cloud,

I floated freely,
bringing
shade and rain
wherever they
were needed.

When I was
a creek,

I flowed effortlessly
around stones
and nourished life
everywhere
I went.

When I was
a seed,

I held
the story
of what

I would become
inside me

until the sun
and rain
let me know
it was time
to share it.

When I was
a flower,

I opened up
to reveal
my beauty
and invited the bees
to share
my sweetness.

Now I am
human

and can do so
many things,

yet I am
full of questions
about who I am
and why I'm here.

Our Big Chance

This is it!

the plants
seem
to be saying,

Our big chance!

Who knows
when we'll have
rain like this
again?

So go ahead
and grow!

Go ahead
and bloom!

Give it all
you've got!

What if
we, too,
could
live
like that?

Water and Stone

Free from shoes
Free from clothes
Free from walls
Free from goals

Flowing
with the river

Basking
with the stones

Feel it
on my skin

Feel it
in my bones

I find
my happy mammal

and know
that I am home.

Wondering About the Mosses

I've been
wondering
about
the mosses.

I know
they've weathered
many dry spells,
come back
from the brink
countless times—

but never
quite like this.

Never
have they had
to wait so long
for a good,
quenching
drink.

Never
has so little rain
fallen
four years
in a row.

I have seen
the mosses
withdraw
into that
shriveled,

apparently lifeless state
and then rise again
to lush, green life
so many times
that I never doubted
they would return.

Their recovery
was at once
miraculous
and predictable.

But recently,
I've been
wondering—

Have we
pushed them
too far?

Will they be able
to come back
from the dry side?

For months
I wonder,

until
the first rain
of the season
reveals
the answer.

I weep
with joy
and relief.

How Can I Walk By?

How can I just walk by
when the delicate green ferns
are unfurling so perfectly?

When the
brave little mosses
are stepping out
in their finest green fronds,

knowing
this is their time
to shine?

When pale gray branches
that have slept all winter
are giving birth
to countless
bright green leaves?

How can I just walk by
without stopping to greet
these beloved friends,
to praise their beauty,
to honor their patient
and generous labors.

I want to bow down
before their humble glory.

I want to kiss the ground
they grow in.

The Birder and the Bird

If we want to know
about birds,

we are taught
to label,
categorize,
count,

to capture
these winged ones
with a few words
or numbers,

reduce them
to a few marks
on a page.

But what
does that teach us
about the essence
of bird-ness—

the wild beating
of wings,

the unbounded freedom
of flight,

the song
that must be sung—

even if no one
is listening?

Poised

A young hawk
stands poised
on the edge
of her nest,

keen eyes
surveying
the wide world
that is
beckoning,

calling her
to leave
the small universe
of twigs and feathers
that is the only world
she has
ever known.

She peers out
at the enticing expanse
of trees and sky,

flaps
her young wings
a few times,

but
does
not
leap.

Somehow
she knows
it is not
yet time—

but soon,
very soon,
it will be.

The place
inside her
that already knows
how to fly
is ready.

GRATITUDE

The Gift of Rain

For the first time
in a long time
it rained today—

each tiny droplet
a gift
to a thirsty plant
or animal.

Seeds say "yes!"
Plants say "yes!"
Parched mosses
say "yes, yes, yes!"

From the tiniest
soil microbe
to the tallest redwood,
we rejoice.

Good Morning

The birds
sound
like I
feel—

thrilled
to behold
the everyday
miracle

of another
sunrise;

eager
to discover
what gifts
the morning
will bring.

Together,
we welcome
the new day.

My heart sings
and flies
with them.

Ninety-three Million

Ninety-three
million miles

is a long way
to travel

to share
your light.

A simple word
or gesture
of thanks

can make it
all worthwhile.

Quenched

This time
last year
I saw
withering,
water-starved
plants everywhere—

their leaves
drooping,
turning brown,
even dying.

I felt
their pain.

Part of me
withered
with them.

But this winter,
it's a different story—

now
we celebrate
the long-awaited
return
of abundant
rainfall.

The plants
drink in
the cool, clear
water.

I drink in
the sight
of lush green leaves,

the scent
of moist dark Earth,

the sound
of flowing water.

We are
quenched.

I Smile at the Rain

I smile at the rain—
even though
it's not exactly
what I had in mind.

I smile at the rain—
even though
I was hoping
it could wait
just a few
more days.

I smile at the rain—
even though
my long-awaited
retreat will be
quite different
with its company...

I may not see
the sun rise
or the moon set
over the mountains,

or the morning sun
moving tenderly
over the bodies
of trees.

I may not hear
the dawn chorus
or the cry of a hawk.

I may not
get to walk
or sit outside
without bundling up
or getting wet
or sometimes both.

Instead,
I will behold
the mosses
in rain-drenched
rapture,

hear the
gentle music
of raindrops
and the
sweet song
of the creek.

And I will feel
the boundless joy
and gratitude
of countless beings
who have been
thirsty for so long,

gently reminding me
that this rain
is a precious gift
welcomed and needed
by many—
including me.

I smile at the rain—
and I mean it!

A Special Day

Today
is a very special day.

Today we celebrate
sun and rain,
light and dark,
the cycles of life,
the great turning
of the wheel.

Today we celebrate
every leaf
on every tree,
every feather
on every bird,
every drop of water
in every stream.

We celebrate
green growing ones
and winged ones,
two-leggeds
and four-leggeds,
all who walk, crawl,
swim, or fly.

We celebrate
each breath of air,
each morsel of food,
each beat of our hearts,
each healthy cell.

We celebrate
the profound miracle
of being alive
in this body
in this moment
on this planet.

Today,
like every other day,
is a very special day.

LOVE AND FRIENDSHIP

An Earthly Personal Ad

Beautiful planet seeks compatible humans
for long-term, committed relationship

Me:

4.5 billion years old (but look younger)
Strikingly beautiful and very well endowed
Highly evolved, intelligent, and accomplished
Head of a large, extended family
Very generous and giving, but don't want to be
   taken advantage of
Seeking a committed but not exclusive relationship

You:

Enjoy forests, mountains, oceans, and diverse
   plants and animals
Very willing to listen and learn (including from
   "other" life forms)
More interested in the common good than
   material wealth
Ready for a long-term, committed partnership
   based on deep love and mutual respect

Interested? Let's connect!

What if...?

What if the leaves,
stirred to singing
by the breeze,
sing with even more joy
when they notice
you are listening?

What if the small white flower
quivers with delight
when you notice
her tiny
yet honorable
contribution
to the beauty
of this world?

And what if
that brief moment
is all she needs
to know that her life
is worth living,
all her efforts
not in vain?

What if the trees
feel the depth
of your pain,
and are quietly
reaching toward you,
offering solace
with everything
they have to give?

What if the whales
diving into the deep blue
can feel your love
for them,
even across all that
open ocean?

What if the water,
weary from
her endless journey,
is replenished by
your gratitude,
which gives her
the strength
to keep going?

What if the Earth
herself
longs to feel
the caress
of your naked feet
on her warm, brown skin?

And what if
the granite mountain,
no matter how remote
and immovable
he may seem,
feels a quiet shiver of joy
when you are touched
by his majestic beauty?

What if...?

Every Leaf

Every drop
of water,

every leaf
on every tree,

every feather
on every bird...

is
full
of
love.

In the Arms of My Beloved

Resting in the arms
of my beloved,
I breathe deep
and easy,

taking refuge
in the sweet peace
of our union.

His quiet, steady presence
and gentle embrace
speak a language
older and deeper
than words,

penetrating the core
of my being
in a way
no human partner
ever has

with the
unmistakable
message that

I am safe,
I am loved,
all is well.

I was so thirsty
for this way
of knowing.

I drink deeply.

I have entered into
the mind
of the tree,
and he
has entered me.

I will never
be alone
again.

Forest Kiss

I kissed a tree today.

It's true,
I'd only known him
a few minutes—

I didn't even
know his name.

Yet I felt drawn to him,
an immediate
sense of connection,
as though we had
known each other
for years.

I was captivated
by his calm
yet powerful presence
and natural good looks.

So when he
reached toward me
with those
supple branches,
how could I resist?

I leaned into him,
lifted my lips,
and tasted
the cool, clear droplets
of rainwater

that clung
to the tender tips
of his branches,

embracing it all—

the cool air,
the gentle rain,
the bright green needles,
the dark and fertile Earth.

Make Love with the Earth

Make love
with the Earth.

Let her
have her way
with you.

Let her caress
your naked feet,
crawl up into your clothes.

Better yet,
slip them off
and let them fall
like leaves
to the ground,

so she can behold
your soft, animal skin,
your naked glory.

Let yourself be undone.

Lie with your belly
on her belly.

Inhale her heady aroma.
Give yourself to her.

Let her mark you
with her rich, fertile scent,
the scent of life itself.

Let her whisper
dark, moist secrets
to you,

awakening
the beautiful
wild animal
slumbering
deep inside you.

Let her
remind you
who
you really are.

EVERYDAY NATURE

A Minor Player

"Did you
grow this?"
my friend asks,

biting into
a juicy, red tomato
from my garden.

"Yes,"
I reply
casually,

as though I had
single-handedly
orchestrated
the remarkable
series of events

that transformed
modest, mild-mannered seeds
into vibrant, voluptuous
vine-ripened tomatoes—

as though I were
director and star
of the vast production
that brought them
to life,

rather than
a minor player
in a miraculous
drama of creation

in which
the plants
are the talented
stars,

the living Earth
the writer and
director,

the sun and water
key supporting players,

and soil microbes
the cast of thousands
that make it
all possible.

My Morning Bath

Every morning,
I take a bath.

I don't
slip off my clothes,
get into a tub,
or use a drop of water.

I simply open my door
and step out
into the new day.

I let the
fresh morning air
flow over my skin,

bathe my eyes
in the living green
of leaves,

soak up
the sweet songs
of birds.

And then,
cleansed
and refreshed,
I move
into the day.

Where Was I?

Where was I
when the first
delicate white petals
of profusion
quietly unfurled
just outside
my front door?

When the
apple tree
across the street
awoke
from her
long hibernation

and bravely
sent forth legions
of blossoms
to meet the light?

Why did
it take
not just one
or 10
but hundreds
of exquisite,
rose-tinged flowers
appearing
before I even noticed
they were in bloom?

What was I thinking?

Could the thoughts
that absorbed
my attention
so completely

possibly have been
more important,
more compelling,
more inspiring

than the arrival
of spring
right on
my doorstep?

Celebration Walk

I went for a walk
to celebrate.

I celebrated having two legs
and the ability to walk.

I celebrated having the freedom
to walk down the street safely
as a woman alone.

I celebrated that bombs were not falling
on me and my neighbors,
and that no one was shooting at us.

I celebrated having had breakfast,
and being able to count on
having lunch and dinner that day,
and pretty much every day
of my life.

I celebrated having plenty
of clean water to drink,
and even enough to take showers
and water my plants,

and not having to walk
for hours every day
carrying a heavy vessel
to retrieve it.

I celebrated sun and rain,
the blooming of flowers,
the songs of birds,
the wisdom of trees,
all the beauty and intelligence
of this generous, green Earth.

I celebrated 48 years
of living and loving,
giving and receiving,
working and playing—
and it wasn't even my birthday.

And after all that,
I celebrated returning home
and having a home to return to.

Ask Your Body

Ask your body
how it wants
to move,
and allow it
to answer
in its own way
and time.

Look past
the mind,
that quick and
clever pupil
in the front row
who invariably
jumps up
and yells out
an answer,

whether or not
you have called
on him,
whether or not
he actually knows.

Look beyond him
to the
quiet student
at the back
of the room

who works
patiently,
tirelessly,
day and night,
accomplishing
great things,

often without
being asked

or noticed

or thanked—

the one with
vast stores
of wisdom
and precious gifts
to share;

the one who
speaks more softly,
yet speaks
the truth.

Give her
a chance
to be heard.

ON THE WILD SIDE

At Home with the Wild Ones

I am at home
in the home
of deer, bobcat,
and coyote,

in some ways more
than in the home
of modern humans.

The lives
of wild ones
make so much sense.

They spend
their days and nights
doing what comes naturally,
doing what needs to be done—

eating,
sleeping,
playing,
learning,

making homes,
making music,
making love.

They do not need medication
to fall asleep
to steady their nerves
to lower their blood pressure
or elevate their mood.

How did we stray
so far from the fold?

When did we forget
how to be
a healthy mammal?

Thoughts on Meeting a Mountain Lion

Like mountain lions,
I love to roam
the remote, scenic trails
of the Central Coast,
unaccompanied
by other members
of my species.

Because we share
these habits,
it is likely
that we will meet
some day.

I look forward
to that moment
with anticipation,
and contemplate
what I will do
when it comes...

Will my skin prickle
with the instinctive knowledge
that I am in the presence
of a mighty predator?

Will I raise my arms,
make myself look
as big as possible,
and yell at the lion,
as the California State Parks
recommend?

Will I loudly chant
a mantra
for rebirth
to a "higher" life form,
as a local
Buddhist retreat center
thoughtfully
suggests?

Or will I
simply meet
the lion
in silent recognition

and with the love,
respect,
and gratitude
that such a magnificent being
deserves?

Sniff the Air Like a Fox

Sniff the air
like a fox,
reading
an invisible map

boldly emblazoned
with lines of scent
that proclaim:
rabbit!
mouse!
coyote!

You say
you don't
know how,
yet something
in you does.

Let yourself travel
back in time,
deep down
through your bones

to the place in you
that still knows
the ancient language,

that still knows how to use
your well-honed senses
to effortlessly read
a rich and complex story
of who passed this way
and when and how.

The Trees Were Not Evacuated

The trees
were not
evacuated.

They stood
their ground.

Even as
smoke
filled the air
and animals
ran for their lives,

they stood
their ground.

Even as
the roar
grew louder
and the heat
unbearable,

they stood
their ground.

Even as
the air filled
with the
terrifying sound
of their
friends and relations
being consumed
by the blaze,

they stood
their ground.

Even as
hot flames
licked
their own bodies,

they stood
their ground.

And even after
they were
reduced to
charred black
skeletons,

still
they
stood
their
ground.

They, too,
lost
everything.

No Matter What

No matter
how hard they try,
they can not
keep us apart.

They can pour concrete
over the rich, dark Earth,
put us in a plastic chair
inside a sheetrock box,
hook us up to electronic devices,
and tell us
we have to stay there all day...

and still we will be
breathing the breath
of towering pines
growing on rugged mountain slopes
and tiny green plankton
floating in distant seas.

And even though
the water we drink
travels through
many miles of pipe,
is doused with chlorine
and may be contained
in plastic bottles...

still we will be drinking water
that has tumbled over granite boulders,
hibernated in frozen lakes,
and reflected the morning sun
from a spider's web.

And even though
the salad we eat
may be grown hundreds of miles away,
harvested and washed
by hands we will never see,
and packaged in a plastic box...

still we will be eating
leaves from plants
whose roots embraced the fertile earth
as their tender green bodies
reached toward the light.

And no matter how relentlessly
we have been trained
to sit still,
to hold our tongues,
to follow the rules
(even when they make no sense),

still we are animals
of flesh and blood,
kin to deer, bear, and whale,
with deep wisdom
in our bones
and untamed passions
in our hearts.

Still there is a wild one inside us,
running barefoot through the forest,
gathering sweet berries,
dancing around the fire,
singing to the moon.

STILLNESS

Seeing the Signs

There
were
signs
all along
the way,

but I
was going
too fast
to read
them.

The
signs
said
"stop."

A Human, Being

Slowly,

gently,

softly.

Not hurrying.

Not pushing.

Not trying
to accomplish
anything
or go anywhere.

Not trying
to be better,
stronger,
or smarter.

Not striving
to attain anything—
even enlightenment.

Just being...

Holding still
so I can find
myself.

Holding still
so the Spirit
can find me.

Seven Days

(Can you imagine...?)

A week
without hurrying.

A week
without deadlines
or schedules;

without hearing
a ringtone
or car alarm,

seeing
a freeway
or store,

or answering
a single
text or email.

A week
of deep,
nourishing
stillness,

moving
slowly and
gently,

following
natural
rhythms.

A week of
being outside
to welcome the sunrise
and bid goodnight
to the sunset;

A week of
being
still enough
to hear
the quiet sounds—

the sigh
of leaves
in the breeze,

the flutter
of birds' wings,

the whispers
of my
own heart,

the
soft stirrings
of poems
asking
to be born.

Moving Forward

If you want

to move forward

skillfully,

slow down.

Breathe.

Allow
your body
and mind
to settle...

peacefully,
effortlessly,

like a soft feather

floating down
through layers
of busy thoughts
and actions,

until at last
you find yourself

resting
in that deep,
still place

where you
can sense
wisdom
flowing

like an
underground river.

Sit by the river,

drink deeply,

and your path
will be clear.

EARTH AND SPIRIT

Humble and Exalted

In the
humble
and exalted
chapel
of my garden,

multitudes gather
to praise life
and celebrate
the miracle of creation.

The choir
starts up early,
even before
the sunrise service,

the birds
openly
confessing
their joys
for all to hear.

The sun
and rain
minister
to the plants;

bees
receive
holy communion
at the altar
of the flowers;

and trees
bestow
gentle benedictions
on all
who gather.

In this sanctuary,
all water is holy,
all ground is sacred,
and all beings
are chosen ones.

Two Prayers

My friend tells me
she is holding me
in her prayers.

I, too,
am holding her
in mine,
which leads me
to wonder...

Do these two prayers
meet somewhere?

And if so,
what happens?

Do they simply
pass each other
on some ethereal plane
and nod politely?

Or do they fall into
a warm embrace,
like dear friends
reunited
after a long absence?

Do they swirl
around each other
for a few moments
like two dancers
and then
gracefully let go?

Or join together
in sacred union
to bring forth
a new creation,
like prayer parents
having a prayer baby?

Or do they flow
in their own
way and time
toward the same
infinite Source,
like rivers flowing
into the ocean,

becoming part
of one great prayer
that touches every shore?

Like a Prayer Flag

with each day
of retreat,
I become
more like
the prayer flags

floating
effortlessly
between
the branches
of the oaks—

filled with
a great
and generous
light,

allowing
everything
to move through,

letting
the breeze
carry
my prayers

wherever
they need
to go.

I Ask Spirit

Over and over,
I hold myself up
to the Spirit
like a newborn baby,

saying...
here I am!
am I good?
am I worthy?
do you love me?

And over and over,
the Spirit surprises me
by answering

yes...
yes...
Yes!

Coming Home

After a long
and sometimes
difficult journey,

I have
finally arrived
at the place
that was waiting
for me all along—
I have come home
to myself.

My Spirit guides
gather 'round,
wrap a warm shawl
around my shoulders,
and say,
"welcome home, child—
we've been waiting
for you."

Now that
I'm finally here,
I wonder
why it took so long—
it all seems
so simple now.

But every step
on that long
and winding path
helped bring me home
to this place.

Leap of Faith

This leap of faith
is not a one-shot deal.

I have not landed
in a warm, soft place
after one easy jump.

I am stepping closer
to the edge
of the chasm,

peering deeper
into the void,

diving farther
into the mystery.

I am leaping again
and again
and again,

feeling the soft, warm air
flowing by me
as I soar
through the darkness,

arms outstretched
like newly-sprouted wings.

And even as I fall
through the
apparently
empty space,

I rest
in the knowledge
that I am guided
by something
much wiser
than myself

that is
taking me
exactly
where
I need to go.

You Don't Have To

You can step into
a church, temple, or mosque...
but you don't have to.

You can
fall on your knees,
finger your beads,
or turn to the East...
but you don't have to.

You can venture out
into the desert alone
for three days
and nights
seeking a vision...
but you don't have to.

You can spend hours
sitting in silence
on a black cushion...
but you don't have to.

You can cover your head
with a lace veil,
a hijab, or a kipa...
but you don't have to.

All you need to do
is turn and face
the Beloved

who has been there
beside you
all along,
patiently waiting
for you to notice...

but you don't have to.

THE NATURE OF CREATION

Poem Delivery

Quiet,
please...

I'm receiving
delivery
of a poem.

As usual,
it is marked:

Urgent

Special Delivery

Open Immediately

Contains Live Poems

I Do Not Know How to Write a Poem

I do not know
how to write
a poem.

I only know
how to
receive one
when it comes—

how to open
the door wide,
offer a cup of tea,

and sit quietly
as it reveals itself
in its own way
and time.

When the Poems Come

The poems come
when I'm quiet.

The poems come
when I'm still.

They come
when I am listening.

The poems come
when they will.

They come
when I'm
not looking,

and in their own
sweet time.

They come
bearing surprises
and hardly ever
rhyme.

Today

Move over, taskmaster.
Move over, critic.

Today is a day
for the muse,
a day for saying "yes!"
to what I love

and "not now, dear'"
to what feels like a burden.

Today, poems
come before to-do lists,
songs before bills,
inspirations
before shoulds.

Today I am free
to wander
through the meadow,
my fingers trailing
through the tall grasses,
enjoying their gentle caress.

Today I am free
to allow the beauty
of a sparrow's trill
to stop me in my tracks.

Time to step through the door
before I hypnotize myself
into thinking
I have to close it.

Time to lift my veil
and allow the muse to
shower me
with sweet kisses.

What Are You Waiting For?

What powerful seeds
lie dormant
deep within you,

longing
to break through
the surface
and reach
their slender stems
toward the light?

What tender buds
are swelling
inside you,

yearning to unfurl
their radiant petals
and reveal their
hidden beauty?

What songs and stories
are swirling
deep within
your breast?

What wild
and magical dreams
are stirring your soul?

What are you
waiting for,
dear one?

The world is hungry
for your beauty,
calling you
to bring forth
your deepest gifts.

The seeds
have been patient
for so long—

waiting
for just a few drops of rain,
a few rays of sun,
a few kind words...
don't deny them that.

Don't wait
until it feels safe
to break open—
that day
may never come.

Shining Your Light

So there you are,
a bright fireball
shining your light
in the midst
of a vast sea
of darkness.

There is nothing
like you
for many
miles around,
for as far
as most eyes
could see.

Still,
you shine
your light
as only you
can do.

You shine
as if your life
depended on it,
because in fact
it does.

You give it
everything
you've got—
fully aware
that you are
giving it all away,

that this giving
eventually
will end your life
as you know it.

You shine
as brightly
as you can,
because
that is what
you are here
to do—

to light up
your corner
of the universe,
to give your gift—
whether or not
anyone can
see it.

You say
it doesn't matter
if anyone notices,

that the pure
act of creation
is enough.

Still,
maybe
one day
on a distant planet,

someone
will gaze up
into the night sky
and notice
your unique spark
of light.

And your light
will enter
and move through them,
stirring something
deep within
that they feel
yet cannot name—

leaving them
subtly
but forever
changed
in a way that
neither they nor you
may ever realize.

And perhaps
this will happen
again and again,
in many places
over many years—

all because
you were willing
to shine your light—

even
if no one
could see it.

ON THE LIGHTER SIDE

Hatching Poems

Like an overprotective
mother hen,
I've been sitting
on an enormous clutch
of poems.

I had no idea
how many
were ready
to hatch.

Yet here
they are,
pecking through
their shells,
stretching
their young wings,

walking around
in the bright light of day,
ready to be seen and heard,
eager to explore
their new world.

Yesterday
they were
confined
to a shell.

Today
they can walk.
Soon
they will fly.

I Speak Chickadee

I speak
a few words
of chickadee—

although
clumsily,
haltingly,
with a thick
human accent.

To a native speaker,
my words may be
completely
unrecognizable.

Doubtless
there are those
who cringe
when they
hear me mangle
the elegant sounds
of their native tongue.

Yet most
seem to
appreciate
my earnest efforts
to learn a few words
of their
beautiful language,
no matter
how awkward
or imperfect.

A Taste of the Wild

I wonder
what he or she
will think—

the field mouse,
wood rat,
or sparrow—

who,
while foraging
for recognizable
and delectable
foods
like seeds
or insects,

stumbles upon
the lone
chocolate chip

I lost
in the tall grass
of their meadow.

Will they
respond with
the field mouse
equivalent of

"wow... this is
the most
incredible thing
I've ever tasted!"

or will it be
more like...
"ewww,
this is
disgusting!
Give me
a succulent grub
instead of this
vile substance
any day!"

Or will the
wayward
chocolate chip,
so far out of its
usual element,
perhaps not even
register
as food,

but rather
as some bizarre,
inedible
substance?

No human
taste bud
can know.

A Good Feet Day

Today
my feet touched

the edge
of the Pacific Ocean,

a sandy beach,

a well-worn trail
through the woods,

a lush carpet
of redwood duff,

the cool waters of
a flowing stream,

the smooth stones
within it,

and the strong body
of a fallen alder tree
that graciously offered
a bridge
across the creek,

inspiring
a spontaneous dance
with gravity.

It was
a good feet day.

Chocolate Meditation

As it happened,
I had just taken
a small bite
of chocolate

at the moment
just before the moment
when the meditation bell rang.

And so the chocolate
rested peacefully
in my mouth
as I rested peacefully
in the moment,

And the sweet morsel
dissolved on my tongue

as one sweet moment
dissolved into the next.

It was a delicious meditation.

POEMLETS

Bare feet
on the Earth

Breathing
in and out

Sound of wind
in the trees

Only this...

and this
is more
than enough.

———————-

I am coming down
from the mountain,

but slowly,
slowly,

and I'm carrying
the mountain
inside me.

———————

The peace
of the forest
overcomes me.

I surrender
willingly.

After a long dry spell,
the creek has found
her voice again.

The rain has
restored
her sweet song.

———

How sweet it is
that trees can
go to sleep
in winter

and wake up
in spring
covered
with blossoms!

———

Can love
keep
a tree
alive?

I don't know,
but I believe
it helps—

water
is good
too.

"Shall we dance?"
asked the wind.

"Yes!"
said the trees.

———

Leaping
from the nest

I see the ground
far below

and give thanks
that my wings
are strong.

———-

Many voices
in the dawn chorus
today.

Some are
familiar—

all are friends.

I've discovered
the secret
to slowing down...

don't
speed up!

————————

I am moving

oh so slowly,

oh so gently.

It's
oh so delicious—

what
I was
hungry for.

————————

"Hold still,"
said the Spirit.

"I have a gift
for you...

but you need
to be still
to receive it."

Tonight
so many words
and images

are gently
imploring me
to give them
a poem to be in.

When they ask
so sweetly,
how can I resist?

———

I am a vessel
blessed by
sacred rivers
of words

that flow
through me
and deposit
fertile soil
along
my banks.

Every moment
is a gift—

sometimes
strangely wrapped,

sometimes
not what we asked for,

yet still a gift.

———

Mother Earth,
I love you.

How can
I serve?

And one final poemlet,
composed by my mother:

Oh, trees!

TIPS AND PRACTICES

Dear reader,

I'm so glad you're here! I was hoping you would visit this section of the book.

One of my deepest intentions in publishing *Poems of Earth and Spirit* is to inspire you to nurture your own connection with nature.

In a world that is often chaotic and challenging, connecting directly and mindfully with nature is one of the best ways to keep ourselves balanced and healthy.

Research confirms what many of us know from experience: nature is profoundly good for our minds, bodies, and spirits. We are happier, healthier, smarter, and kinder when we spend time in nature. It restores us to health and wholeness like nothing else. And no wonder—it's where we evolved. It's what we're designed for. It's our original home and habitat.

No matter who you are, where you live, or what you struggle with, you are fully capable of enjoying a nourishing and healing connection with the natural world. It is in *your* nature to connect with nature. It is your birthright.

And this is not just about feeling good or staying healthy. Connecting with nature also impacts how we treat others and the Earth. It makes us more creative, more cooperative, and more motivated to protect our precious planet. If each of us spent a little more time with our feet on the dirt and our faces in the breeze, we could create a more peaceful and thriving world.

There are two basic keys to nurturing your relationship with nature amidst the challenges of modern life: finding simple ways to connect with the Earth wherever you are, and understanding how to open to a deeper communion when you are in natural settings. This chapter can help you do both.

Think of it as a small treasure chest, overflowing with gems that can help you tune into the peace and healing of nature wherever you are. You can take out one gem at a time, hold it up to the light and enjoy it for a while, and then choose another when you're ready. Or you can sift through all of them, notice which ones catch your eye, and take a few along on your next nature outing. Better yet, carry this book out into the meadows and forests and see where the poems and practices lead you.

In order to meet you where you are, this chapter is organized into two sections.

Ten Ways to Deepen Your Connection When You're in Nature: These are crafted for places where nature's design is more primary, and times when you have stepped away from your everyday life into a space of greater freedom and flexibility. They focus on cultivating a deeper communion with nature by slowing down, opening your senses and awareness, being present, and engaging more directly with the natural world.

Ten Ways to Connect with Nature in Daily Life: These are designed for places with more buildings and people, and days with more demands and distractions. They emphasize simple ways to notice and appreciate trees, birds, water, and other aspects of the natural world that are common in built environments, and to integrate mindful nature connection with daily activities.

Of course, humans live in a wide range of settings and with a wide range of schedules. The tips for daily life are tailored for busy people in cities and suburbs. If you live in a natural setting or have more ease in your schedule, many of the tips for deepening your connection may also work in your everyday life.

Both sections include ten general tips. The daily life section also includes suggestions linked to specific times of the day and common activities. You'll see that there is some overlap between the two sections, including a few of the same tips, but they are framed differently for the different settings.

May these tips and practices bring more peace, joy, and balance into your days and into our world.

Ten Ways to Deepen Your Connection When You're in Nature

1. Unplug.

When you go into nature, you have a precious opportunity to unhook from the endless distractions of the virtual world and nourish mind, body, and spirit. Unplugging from electronic devices will help you release stress, attune to the rhythms of nature, and be more fully present with the peace and beauty around you. See what it's like to leave your phone behind and experience the natural world without an electronic filter. If you do bring a device along, turn it off or silence it, stow it away, and use it as little as possible.

2. Be present.

When you're truly present in nature, you're more available to receive the abundant gifts that await you. As you enter a natural setting, take a few moments to notice where you are and give yourself a chance to arrive. Sit or stand quietly and open your awareness to what's around you. Enjoy a few deep breaths. Feel your feet on the Earth. Sense yourself in your body and in that place.

As you hike or move through the landscape, practice bringing mindful awareness to the sights and sounds around you and your experience in the moment. Notice what draws your attention. Pause to breathe it in, or lean in for a closer look. See how fully present you can be with a single leaf, a flowing creek, or the warmth of sun on your skin. Know that simply being in nature is healing, and that the more present you are, the more you will receive.

3. Open your senses.

Your senses are gateways to the natural world, and when they are open you can experience it more fully. Practice tuning into your senses one at time. Savor the delicious sights, sounds, scents, and textures of nature—perhaps even flavors if you can do so safely. Try exploring a tree, flower, or small patch of Earth with all your senses, drinking it in as you might an exquisite performance or healing touch. Or close your eyes, open your ears, and enjoy the gentle music of birdsong, moving water, or leaves whispering in the wind. Literally get in touch with nature by mindfully exploring the varied textures of trees, water, stone, and more. Use your hands, bare feet, or your whole body. Bring your full awareness to what you are touching—and what is touching you!

4. Expand your range of motion.

Movement is a potent language that speaks volumes about our relationship to our surroundings. By bringing more awareness to how we move and expanding our movement vocabulary, we can engage with nature with greater aliveness, creativity, and joy.

Explore different ways of walking: barefoot, slowly, quietly. Bring awareness to each step. Try moving less like a train on a track and more like a curious wild animal—climb a tree, wander through a stream bed, or clamber over boulders.

Rather than just moving *through* the landscape, move *with* it. Engage directly with the beings and elements around you—say hello with a friendly touch, meander and notice where you feel drawn to go, or allow nature's movements to inspire your own. Enter into a more dynamic and embodied conversation with the living world, letting your body language affirm connection rather than separation. Let yourself be moved.

5. Slow down.

If you're constantly on the move, you'll cover a lot of ground, but also miss a lot of what's happening around you. But if you slow down or stop, new worlds will open up to you. Try gently exploring an intriguing spot at a very leisurely pace, and see how much beauty and wonder you can encounter in one small area. When you're out for a hike, discover the power of the pause—stop, look, and listen, for a moment, a minute, or more. If you're ready for a deeper dive into stillness, sit quietly and enjoy simply being present in one place, bathing in the sights and sounds of nature. Or find a peaceful spot to lie down, let your mind and body release into the support of the Earth, and practice the quietly radical art of resting. Discover how much can come to you when you hold still.

6. Listen deeply.

Listening is a powerful act, essential to any kind of relationship—including with the natural world. When you're quiet, you're more available to listen. Walk or sit in silence for a while, tuning into the sounds of nature. Practice being quiet inside and out, and allow the natural world to speak to you. See if you can engage without a specific agenda and let the land lead you—or you can hold a question or intention and see what comes to you. Notice what draws your attention and where you feel called to go or stop. Or sit still with a pen and journal, open yourself to natural inspiration, and discover what wants to come through. (You may want to have a special journal dedicated to your nature experiences and reflections.) See if you can listen not just with your ears, but also at a more subtle level with your body, heart, and spirit. Nature holds abundant wisdom for those who listen deeply.

7. Go solo.

Humans are fascinating creatures who tend to absorb a lot of attention when they are near. Going "solo" allows you to see, hear, and feel more of the natural world, including birds and other creatures. Alone, you discover wonders you would have missed if you were with other people, especially talkative ones. Solitude in nature allows you to cultivate deeper connections with more-than-human beings, and with yourself.

Try a solo walk or sit in a place where you feel comfortable. Or if you prefer to go out with others, try going "solo-ish"—sit or walk a short distance apart for a while, and then reconnect with your companions to share about your experiences. When you're out in nature, you're never truly alone.

8. Make friends.

Making friends with "other" beings and natural places is easier than you may think, and more like making friends with people than you might expect. It starts with simply knowing it is possible and giving these natural friendships a chance to blossom. Notice which beings or places you are instinctively drawn to. Give yourself a chance to get to know them, preferably one on one. Sit quietly with them, touch them, speak to them, listen to them. Even a simple "hello" or "thank you" can establish a stronger bond.

Tend the connection as you might with human friends or romantic interests—make dates to get together, be curious about them, show them you care. You may be surprised to discover the depth and quality of love and friendship that can grow. And even when you're apart, you can communicate with your nature allies and call on them for support.

9. Honor the sacred.

We humans have an inherent longing to connect with something greater than ourselves, and nature offers perhaps the most effortless and enjoyable path to that communion. Honoring the sacredness of nature is a powerful way to deepen our innate bond with the Earth and all life—and to remember our own true nature.

You don't need to follow a script or go about it a certain way. There is tremendous power in authentic, heartfelt blessings and ceremonies, even very simple and spontaneous ones. You can honor a special being or place in nature with a song, poem, prayer, or words of gratitude. Or you can make a symbolic offering or create a ceremony to thank or bless a tree, river, or mountain— on your own or with others. If you have a regular spiritual or mindfulness practice, try bringing it outside and welcoming the natural world into your practice, or including nature in your practice wherever you are.

10. Give thanks.

When we're out in nature, we receive many gifts—both tangible ones like beauty, shade, and berries, and less tangible ones like peace, healing, and inspiration. Expressing gratitude helps us enjoy and appreciate these gifts more fully and deepens our connection with nature. Try saying "thank you" to some of the beings and elements that give to you—naming names is good! ("Thank you lake, sun, chickadees...")

Developing simple customs, like giving thanks as you get up from a lunch spot or complete a hike, will help you make a habit of gratitude. You might also consider giving back to a special place by removing trash or volunteering.

Ten Ways to Connect with Nature in Daily Life

1. Start where you are.

Notice how the natural world is part of your everyday life, even in the midst of a city—in food, water, plants, animals, daily and seasonal cycles, your own body, and more. Simply bringing awareness to the presence of nature around you will strengthen your connection. Notice which aspects of nature you are instinctively drawn to, and find ways to say "yes" to them, even just for a few moments.

2. Go screen-free.

Take breaks from electronic devices, especially when you're outside. Turn off or silence your device, put it away, or (better yet) leave it behind so you can unhook the electronic leash and be more fully present. Enjoy observing and exploring the world around you, tuning into the presence of plants, birds, clouds, and other natural beauty.

3. Go for the green and blue.

Look for opportunities to be near trees, plants, and water, and to notice and appreciate their company. Choose walking, biking, and driving routes with more green and blue. Eat some of your meals outside and/or near plants or water. Grow a garden or bring living plants into your home and work space. Gaze softly at green plants (indoors or out) for quick breaks, and venture out into green space for longer breaks.

4. Bring it outside.

Begin with something you already do, bring it out to a park or beautiful outdoor setting, and you'll enhance your enjoyment and the health benefits. A few great options: exercise, meals, reading, writing, yoga, meditation, and sharing time with friends or family. Or simply step outside during the day, feel the sun or breeze on your skin, take in the sights and sounds, and notice what draws your attention in a pleasing way.

5. Bring the outside in.

Having nature images or natural treasures in your indoor environment or visualizing yourself in a peaceful outdoor setting will help you stay connected with nature and the special places you love. You'll also receive some of the physical and mental health benefits of actually being in those places.

6. Move your body.

Your own body is a natural wonder. Movement is essential to keep it happy and healthy and to support your natural intelligence and vitality. Exercising outside quickly multiplies the benefits and motivates you to keep moving—even just a brief walk makes a difference. Find opportunities to move your body regularly, daily if possible—especially ones that take you outdoors or bring you joy.

7. Make friends.

Walk or bike around your neighborhood or sit quietly outside and meet your natural neighbors, observing them with friendly curiosity. You might be surprised to discover how many fascinating more-than-human neighbors you have. Notice if there are particular trees, animals, or natural places you feel drawn to. Find ways to communicate and tend your connection with them. They can become dear friends and powerful allies if you give them a chance.

8. Give thanks.

Every day, we receive many beautiful and useful gifts from the natural world, mostly without noticing. Look for opportunities to appreciate these gifts more, even just for a few moments. You might pause to give thanks for a meal, a sunset, or a lovely flower. Consider keeping a gratitude journal or writing a thank-you letter to the Earth or to a plant, animal, or place that is special to you. The more you feel and express your gratitude, the more it will nourish you.

9. Connect and conserve.

Your daily lifestyle choices can strengthen your connection with nature and protect it at the same time by getting you outside, using human and green power, and reducing resource consumption. A few examples: biking or walking rather than driving; using a clothesline instead of a dryer; eating local, seasonal, wild, and/or organic foods; gardening and growing some of your own food; and composting. Linking these daily actions with love for the Earth makes them more satisfying and meaningful.

10. Make it part of your day.

Integrating your nature connection practices with regular events or times of day makes them more doable and reminds you to do them. You might pause to greet a tree that you walk by on your way to work, visit your garden for a few minutes when you come home, or thank the plants and animals who made your dinner possible. Consider this an essential wellness practice to integrate into your day, like eating meals or brushing your teeth. A little bit of mindful nature connection, even in the midst of a city, can go a surprisingly long way.

Here are some examples of how to integrate nature connection with everyday life, based on the above tips:

<u>In the early morning...</u>
- Greet the day. Notice the sunrise, sky, and weather. Take a few deep breaths and perhaps give thanks or affirm your intentions for the day.
- Step outside, breathe in the air, and take in the sights and sounds. Notice if birds or other natural neighbors are out and about.
- If you have a garden, visit your plants and see what they're up to, and maybe water or tend them a bit.
- Go for a walk or exercise outdoors. You'll think and feel better during the day and sleep better at night.
- Do a nature meditation or visualization. You can use a recording or simply picture yourself in a peaceful, beautiful setting; tune into what you see, hear, and feel around you; and drink it in.
- If you're cultivating relationships with particular allies in the natural world, you can call them in, thank them for their gifts, and invite their support and guidance.

<u>During the work day...</u>
- Include living plants, natural objects, or nature images in your workspace, in places where you will see them regularly.

- Take actual breaks so you can return to your tasks with renewed energy, focus, and creativity—even micro-breaks make a difference. (Be aware: looking at a screen is not a real break!)
- For brief breaks, look up from your work or device and focus softly on something natural or beautiful—an indoor plant or nature image, or trees or clouds outside the window. If you've been sitting, stand up and stretch or move around.
- For longer breaks, walk or move your body, ideally in a setting with green plants, water, or other natural elements. Take meal breaks outside or near a window with a view when you can.

While you're walking outside...
- Turn off your device or leave it behind and notice your surroundings. Your walk will be safer, more enjoyable, and more revitalizing.
- Open your senses and awareness and explore the world around you. Look up, down, and all around. Notice and enjoy what's happening in the present moment—you may discover unexpected delights.
- Try on different routes to your usual spots—make it a mini-adventure!
- Tune into the presence of the natural world around you. Notice seasonal changes like the first spring blossoms or fall colors. Greet some of your natural neighbors—smile at a bird or say hello to a tree.
- Spot beauty, even in small things or unlikely places. Pause to appreciate a lovely flower, plant, or butterfly and let it nourish you.
- Marvel at everyday wonders of the world like plants growing, birds flying, and dewdrops making rainbows in the sun.

<u>While you're driving or traveling...</u>
- Choose routes with more plants, trees, or water, ideally without increasing your carbon footprint.
- Tune into the presence of nature when it's safe to do so. While you're at a red light or stuck in traffic, see if you can find something natural or beautiful to look at. (Give those median plants some love!)
- When you arrive somewhere, take in your surroundings, noticing the presence of the natural world.

<u>At mealtimes...</u>
- Before you enjoy a meal, pause to notice the food on your plate and the abundance it represents. As you eat, appreciate the flavors, textures, and aromas.
- Picture the plants, animals, and people who made your meal possible and send them some gratitude.
- Speak words of thanksgiving for your meal, your day, and your companions, or share a nature connection moment from your day.

<u>Near the end of the day...</u>
- Notice the sunset, the moon, and the night sky. Step or sit outside to observe them and feel the night air.
- Give thanks for some of the gifts you received from the Earth that day.
- Journal or share with a loved one about something you're grateful for, or a nature experience from your day.
- Do a nature meditation or visualization (see early morning tips).
- Read a few poems (perhaps from the book you are holding in your hands) or a story that invites you into the natural world.

CLOSING WORDS

Many Thanks!

"All creation is co-creation."
—Marcia Conner

Many beings helped make this book possible—literally a cast of thousands. I am grateful to them all and want to acknowledge some of them here...

The trees, plants, animals, streams, and other beings who generously shared their inspiration and wisdom, taught me to listen in new ways, and became some of the best friends I've ever had. (Even if you can't read this, you know who you are!)

Special places in the natural world I returned to again and again to restore my senses and connect with something deeper, especially the North Coast of Santa Cruz, Rancho Del Oso, Wilder Ranch, Laguna Creek, the Big Sur Coast, the Yuba River, and Kings Canyon.

Suzanne Morrow, Terra and Scott Collier-Young, and Noël Vietor and Fletcher Tucker for offering their places on the land as havens for listening and writing.

The Vajrapani Institute for creating sacred space to receive the abundant gifts that come in silence, and providing fertile conditions for the birth of many poems.

The spirit guides and allies who have supported me more than I will ever know, and Cathy Pedevillano for helping me learn to work across the realms of Earth and Spirit.

Fellow travelers in the world of deep nature connection for sharing ideas and encouragement, especially Ariana Candell, Kathren Murrell Stevenson, Carolyn Brown, Collette Streight, Noël Vietor, and Fletcher Tucker.

Debora Seidman for helping me honor the sacredness of writing and trust my deeper voice.

Mary Reynolds Thompson for skillful advice and support with many aspects of writing, editing, publishing, and marketing.

Christi Voenell for her exquisite original drawings, understanding the essence of *Poems of Earth and Spirit* from the very start, and being a joy to work with every step of the way.

Jeremy Thornton for the gorgeous cover design, Alistair Scott for the stunning cover image, and Mária Kersey for the author photo.

Kathy McClure for patient and skillful help with navigating CreateSpace and formatting.

Extra helpings of gratitude for those who reviewed and proofed copious amounts of text: Connie Habash, Jared Jones, Jay Siedenburg, Joanna Jarvis, Nina Siedenburg, and Tamara Myers. Thanks also to Andrew Davis, Ariana Candell, Carroll La Fleur, Joel Wallock, Krista Holt, and Paul Machlis for additional text review and proofing.

The "Circle of Friends" who added welcome reinforcements to my shoestring publishing budget and cheered me on along the way. (See names on page 138.)

Others who supported this project in various ways: Dan Marston, Kieran Kennedy, Michael Levy, James Gronvold, Hamsa Merlet, and Matt Perry.

The skilled healers who helped restore health and balance to my body, especially Curtis Cramblett, Brie Wieselman, Mudita Voigt, and Kate Robbins.

Heather Houston, Yala Lati, and the Dance Church community for keeping me singing and dancing as I climbed the mountain of book completion.

Everyone who has ever loved me, believed in me, encouraged me, and reflected my goodness to me— fortunately too numerous to list here!

And to anyone else I should have acknowledged here but didn't, humble and heartfelt thanks!

Finally, a deep bow of gratitude to my ancestors and especially my parents, Nina and Jay Siedenburg and "bonus mom" Pauline Siedenburg, who helped make it all possible. I couldn't have done it, or anything, without you.

For all my relations (Mitakuye Oyasin), and for the benefit of all beings.

Circle of Friends for *Poems of Earth and Spirit*

Alan Voegtlen
Annette Barnett
Ariana Candell
Carroll La Fleur
Cathy Pedevillano
Connie Habash
Curtis Cramblett
Dave and Mary Anne
 Kramer-Urner
Devi Peri
Donna Scheifler
Erica DeGarmo
Erin Ramsden
Jared Jones
Jennifer Alexander
Joanna Jarvis
Kris Ayer
Krista Holt

Letitia Schwarz Velasquez
Livia Hart
Marcia Heinegg
Mari Cope
Mária Kersey
Maureen Harrahy
Megan Hawk
Mike Fullmer
Mitchell Goldstein
Nadine Golden
Shari Rose
Steve Lustgarden
Sunny Skys
Susan Kauffman
Tamara Myers
Terry Teitelbaum
(plus 10 anonymous
donors)

About the Author

Kai Siedenburg is a nature connection guide, Ecotherapist, writer, and poet based in Santa Cruz, CA. A pioneer in integrating nature connection and mindfulness as a path to mind-body wellness, Kai is passionate about helping people to cultivate mindful, intimate, and healing relationships with the natural world wherever they are. She offers group and individual programs through Our Nature Connection.

Her work is co-created with the natural world—guided by the generous wisdom of trees, mountains, water, and stone—and infused with love for people and the Earth. It is also informed by 30-plus years of professional experience developing innovative educational programs and by extensive personal practice in mindfulness, holistic healing, and creative expression.

Kai's writings about nature connection and human-Earth relations comprise a large volume of poems, practices, and essays, as well as a draft nature connection workbook for modern humans. She welcomes opportunities to share her work more widely. *Poems of Earth and Spirit* is her first book.

Kai loves to find herself out on the Earth, in her garden, in water, or on the dance floor. You can find her at OurNatureConnection.com.

About the Illustrator

Christi Voenell finds magic in the natural world and tries to capture this feeling in her art. She gathers inspiration from moments when she has been able to slow down and experience nature—such as visiting tide pools with her mother as a child, spending a summer on an isolated island studying wild orcas, and her time guarding young peregrine falcons she helped release in the Sierra Nevada mountains.

As an artist Christi works in multiple media, but her favorite is collage. She is a writer who loves poetry and practices Buddhist meditation. She works at UC Santa Cruz, where she graduated with a degree in Environmental Studies.

About TreeSisters

Imagine a reforestation revolution ignited by the shared creativity and courage of a global network of millions of women.

TreeSisters is a non-profit organization aiming to radically accelerate tropical reforestation by engaging the unique feminine consciousness, gifts, and leadership of women everywhere and focusing it towards global action.

TreeSisters is planting over a million trees a year, and is now calling for women to plant a billion trees a year, by becoming a treesister and contributing monthly to tropical reforestation.

A portion of the sales of this book raises funds in aid of TreeSisters.

TreeSisters.org

About Our Nature Connection

Our Nature Connection inspires people to connect directly and mindfully with nature as a path to happier, healthier lives and a more peaceful planet.

We empower people to:
- find simple ways to connect with the Earth in daily life,
- cultivate intimate, nourishing, and respectful bonds with the natural world, and
- access nature-based healing for mind, body, and spirit.

Our work is a gentle yet powerful integration of deep nature connection, mindfulness practice, and holistic healing—a unique approach we call *NatureWise*. We offer group programs, individual sessions, and consulting services for your benefit and the benefit of all beings.

OurNatureConnection.com

Resources for Deepening Your Connection with Nature

OurNatureConnection.com

Visit our website for tips, articles, and poetry that bring you closer to nature and nature closer to you. Join our e-mail list to receive monthly infusions of nature-based goodness.

Home-Based Program: The Path of Nature Connection

Tap into the power of nature to create a happier, healthier, more meaningful life with this engaging, experiential six-week course. Discover how cultivating your personal connection with nature brings greater ease and balance into daily life; frees up energy and creativity; and heals mind, body, and spirit. Includes six group calls to inspire and guide your practice; easy, enjoyable "home play" choices for both cities and wild places; and options for group and individual support.

Group Nature Immersion Programs

Awaken your senses and discover what it's like to connect more intimately and mindfully with the natural world. Learn the surprisingly simple keys to accessing more profound peace, joy, and healing in nature. Leave feeling relaxed, replenished, and more fully at home in yourself and on the Earth—and with simple tools you can use to connect with nature anytime and anywhere. (Half-day, daylong, and multi-day options.)

Individual Sessions

Face life's challenges with greater clarity and ease through skilled, personalized support. Learn how to receive healing and guidance from the natural world, activate your innate wisdom and creativity, and cultivate a more nourishing connection with nature that supports you wherever you are. (Available via phone, Zoom, Skype, or in person.)

Consulting Services

Enliven and empower your professional work by tapping into nature's capacity to calm, heal, and inspire, even while you're indoors. We can teach you simple yet potent practices to share with your clients; help you design and lead nature-based experiences; or craft a custom program to reduce stress, promote wellness, spark creativity, or meet other goals for your organization.

Our Next Book—Coming in Early 2020:
Space Between the Stones: Poems of Earth and Spirit Volume 2

Like the original *Poems of Earth and Spirit,* this new collection reflects a quiet yet passionate love affair with the natural world and a friendly fluency with everyday spirituality. Intimate original poems and simple yet potent practices invite us to step out of the frantic swirl of the modern world and into a realm in which all life is intelligent, all beings are our kin, and we are all naturally creative.

Learn more about these resources at OurNatureConnection.com